ITALIAN
SCULPTURE
from Prehistory to the Etruscans

Massimo Carrà

ITALIAN SCULPTURE

from Prehistory to the Etruscans

CASSELL
LONDON

Cassell Publishers Limited
Artillery House, Artillery Row
London SW1P 1RT

Translated by Timothy Paterson from the Italian original
Dai nuraghi agli Etruschi. La scultura minore nell'Italia preromana

© Gruppo Editoriale Fabbri, Bompiani, Sonzogno, Etas S.p.A., Milan 1966,
1984

This edition 1988

British Library Cataloguing in Publication Data

Carrà, Massimo
Italian sculpture. — (Cassell's styles in art).
1. Italian sculptures, to ca. 500 BC
I. Title   II. Dai Nuraghi agli Etruschi. *English*
730'.945

ISBN 0-304-32175-3

Printed in Italy by Gruppo Editoriale Fabbri, Milan

CONTENTS

Page

CIVILISATION AND ART IN ANCIENT ITALY

The ethnographic picture of primitive Italy is extremely complex since the country became the goal of two distinct migrations: the great continental migration across the Alpine valleys from Central and Eastern Europe, and the migration by sea across the Mediterranean.

It is thought that the first peoples to arrive were the Ligurians and Sicels (the latter passing through Latium and southern Italy before settling in Sicily, followed by the Sicans and Sardinians, who perhaps shared common Ligurian and Iberian origins intermixed with Tyrrhenian and African elements. Originally, the various Italic peoples coming from the distant lands of Eurasia were of a distinct continental character, farmers and shepherds rather than sailors – a fact that was to influence later events in Italy. Thus were laid the ethnic foundations of Italy, giving rise to a number of different Apenninic and coast-dwelling cultures.

The earliest finds date back to the Old Stone Age. Although fragmentary, they are still sufficient to establish the existence of spiritual activity already being expressed through the medium of art. This art was closely connected with, or perhaps even subjected to, practical ends. The value of art for its own sake was appreciated only after the development of the great urban civilisations; for aesthetic activity was a luxury that man could barely afford in his struggle for survival.

Contemporary with numerous implements, almond-shaped axes, chipped flint, scrapers, and early ornaments in bone or shell, are smooth stones engraved with rudimentary geometrical patterns clearly of magical significance. There are also graffiti, discovered in caverns at Levanzo, Addaura and Niscemi in Sicily, depicting various animals, in a realistic manner in no way inferior to that of the similar but better-known graffiti in caves of the Cantabrian Mountains in Spain. Moreover, at Addaura near Palermo, man is already represented in a group of figures drawn on different planes, which suggests that the primitive artist was trying his hand at rudimentary composition.

At about the same time the various proto-Italic peoples began to participate in the statuette-making culture spreading over the whole of Europe from Russia to the Atlantic. Although the number of statuettes found in Italy is somewhat smaller than elsewhere, both the subjects and the treatment are almost identical with other European pieces, suggesting a common process of evolution and a common approach to art and religion. Sculpture is restricted to crude figurines of women, their proportions distorted in order to emphasise their sexual functions. The purpose of this was both ritual and propitiatory; above all, these Venuses with their rounded buttocks glorify fertility. The Italian examples were discovered in various places all over the country, including the caves of the Balzi Rossi in Liguria. Of particular interest as regards quality of expression are the two figurines found at Savignano sul Panaro and Chiozza in Emilia; both are of unusual dimensions (the former 22·5 cm high, the latter 20.5 cm) and are inspired by an anatomical realism that is successfully combined with the customary symbolic exaggeration of proportions.

The appearance of sharp polished stone axes marks the advent of the New Stone Age in Italy. Living conditions improved and habits became less primitive. The transition from a hunting and fishing civilisation to one based on cultivation and stock-breeding increased man's belief in a superhuman world, for the peasant depends too much on natural phenomena not to see in them the presence of forces before which he feels inadequate and impotent.

In the earliest agricultural civilisations the death-cult, aimed at regeneration, bears witness to Neolithic man's belief in an after-life, and serves to indicate his relationship with the universe. Henceforward corpses were arranged in a foetal position and placed in caverns or ditches surrounded by stones. Around them was set an array of symbolical objects – weapons, pottery and small benign idols – as an act of homage towards their departed souls, or perhaps as a precaution against their suddenly returning to life.

The world of the dead was distinctly separate from that of the living. By trapping and fixing the likeness of the dead in carved stone images, or by setting against them adverse, symbolic forces, it was thought that both death and the evil spirits connected with it could be warded off. Symbolism is one of man's earliest inventions. A zigzag line, for example, symbolises water, and a branch symbolises vegetation; and together they represent fertility – that is, the force in opposition to death. Figurines of the Mother Goddess are also symbolic of life (even when the anatomy is reduced to breasts and pubic triangles) as are figures of nude women; of all effigies, these are most frequently found in funerary ware.

Objects unearthed in Neolithic burial-grounds are more varied in shape and naturally more refined in concept than those of the Old Stone Age. New conditions and a wider consciousness produced a very different form of art: whereas the old culture adhered to the faithful representation of real objects, men of the new culture proved able to realise a more profound and idealised sense of reality. With this, stamped or chromic pottery first made its appearance, and the long history of applied art began.

The main consequence of maritime trading, a revolutionary factor in man's existence, was the importation of copper into Europe from Asia Minor. In Italy, copper replaced the widespread use of stone over a transitional period which differed in length from region to region. In southern Italy, and especially in Sicily (areas exposed to Greek and Anatolian influences by reason of their geographical position) there was a relatively rapid evolution. This is also evident in pottery, by now flourishing, which was decorated with black geometrical patterns on a red ground that were used over and over again. In northern Italy, more closely tied to European continental civilisation, the transition from stone to copper was far slower; finds of crude pottery, weapons and implements from sites in Lombardy reveal a stubborn persistance in the use of traditional forms and material; copper objects appear only sporadically.

Tin was imported into Europe from Cornwall via the Atlantic coast of France. Once importation had been increased and methods of alloying tin with copper improved, a new metal – harder and stronger than copper, and suitable for the casting of implements and weapons – came into use: bronze. Despite the great distances separating the Mediterranean basin from the centres producing the components of bronze, the metal spread throughout the area with extraordinary rapidity; possibly because further widespread developments in maritime trading took place at the same time.

The unity of culture in Italy during the New Stone Age now disintegrated. In the Po Valley, lake-dwelling and *terramara* civilisations were developing. These were settlements built on piles out of the water's reach. Here the death-cult (always a great help in interpreting any culture) was based upon cremation. Beside each settlement stood its necropolis, also built on piles, a storehouse of crude earthenware urns and only small quantities of funerary ware.

Along the Apennines and in southern Italy there are no traces of *terramara* settlements. Both megalithic structures and cliff dwellings, which may be directly linked with those of the Copper Age, demonstrate the existence of totally different living conditions and, in all probability, a totally different cultural history. Dolmens are also to be found in both Apulia and Sardinia. They are more or less cube-shaped and built of large stone slabs, and were used as either dwellings or tombs. (If the latter, the old inhumation rites were still adhered to). Moreover both dolmens and stone huts are a valuable source of funerary ware and household objects. In Apulia there is a further curious piece of artistic evidence, namely a kind of obelisk, similar to the menhir of northern France.

Sicily was already feeling the influence of Aegeo-Cretan civilisation. The necropolis at Castelluccio, near Noto, has furnished by far the best documentation of past life in the island. Its relationship with Minoan art and architecture is striking, especially as regards certain typical decorative patterns (for instance, the double spiral), an elegant taste in ornamentation (small bone plaques carved in relief), pottery, and even weapons. Some finds, on the other hand, are free from Eastern influence; there is, for example, a bell-shaped drinking-glass of Iberian pattern which indicates the existence of a second stream of economic and cultural exchanges with the West. That exchanges in fact took place seems further borne out by the decorative carving on a tomb door in the museum at Syracuse, which has a certain affinity not only with Minoan models, but also with reliefs carved on menhirs in France.

In Sardinia the multiple characteristics of Bronze

Age civilisation are far more marked, its lasting monument being the *nuraghe,* a cone-shaped tower. The production of bronze objects gradually developed, including weapons, implements and the famous figurines.

We have now passed from the prehistoric to the historic, or at least proto-historic, age. It was during this phase that the first ethnic groups to settle in Italy at the time of the Old Stone Age were supplanted by other Indo-European peoples who had arrived over the Alpine passes and across the Mediterranean. Italy acquired a definite ethnic physiognomy; the various peoples who had led a nomadic existence, roaming over the Balkans and Central Europe towards the end of the 2nd millennium BC, now settled there, amalgamating more or less smoothly with the local populations. Each of these newly arrived races had its own particular traditions and characteristics. Centres of civilisation differing among themselves were thus formed, though no longer with a *lingua franca,* and were destined to flourish until at least halfway through the 1st millennium BC.

The different localities chosen by the new races are interesting. In northern Italy the Venetic group originating from Eastern Europe settled at Este. In the central regions were the Picene and Sabellic peoples of

Illyrian stock, and the Villanovan culture. The latter, probably Umbrian in origin, flourished in the Apennines between the 10th and 5th centuries BC; Etruscan civilisation was later to be grafted on to it. Iapygians, Daunians and Messapians populated the south, while across the water in Sicily were the Sicels. (By the 8th century BC both Sicily and southern Italy had been colonised by the Chalcidians and Corinthians, with the result that a culture very different from those in north-central Italy was formed). The proto-Sardinians thrived in Sardinia; they were a singular, isolated people whose customs and art forms appear to have few affinities with those of other Mediterranean countries. It is to them that we must now turn our attention.

NURAGHIC BRONZE FIGURINES

The 19th-century archaeologists who first became interested in the *nuraghi* – the mysterious and somewhat sinister towers scattered throughout the Sardinian countryside – were inclined to associate them with the Western megalithic culture. Later discoveries, excavations and earth-stratum surveys have, however, proved that both farming civilisation and metallurgy began in the Aegean and Near East; and the theory of the primary, autonomous character of Western megalithic civilisation has therefore been abandoned. Now that the origins of European culture have been reduced to a single source, the *nuraghi* are considered to be the somewhat late product of an encounter between Western and Eastern styles of architecture, not without a certain humble, barbarised affinity with the great traditions of Egyptian building. ('Eastern' is used throughout this book to describe the Eastern Mediterranean and Near East).

Away from the centres of progress, the isolated Sardinians were not affected by the influence of the then rapidly spreading Eastern civilisations.

The more open communal way of life flourishing elsewhere in the Mediterranean was totally lacking in Sardinia, where temples, theatres, stadia, meeting- and market-places had yet to be built. Today it is believed that the oldest *nuraghi* date from the end of the 2nd millennium BC, though village life as such became established only with the progress made in extracting metals from their ores and the subsequent working of them; after which village life flourished until the Roman conquest in the 3rd century BC, which interrupted the further development of Sardinian civilisation.

A little under seven thousand *nuraghi* are still to be

found. Perched high above mountain passes or else scattered along the sea-coast, they suggest that their occupants belonged to a feudal warrior society with its roots in the land; though it could not have been entirely cut off from international commerce since tin and copper at least were imported to alloy bronze.

It is a curious, though not completely inexplicable fact that traces of man's presence during the Old and New Stone Ages are almost entirely lacking. Evidence of the Copper Age exists in the oven-shaped sepulchres *(domus de janus)* discovered at Gallura and in the countryside around Cagliari; and also in the dolmen-like structures on the highlands in the north-central region of the island, where the prevalently Ibero-Almerian cultural derivations bear witness to ancient links with the more conspicuous centres of Western civilisation. Together with the large, varied assortment of funerary and votive pottery, some of which are decidedly novel in form and decoration, are the nude figurines which may be attributed to the same period. They are made in basalt or limestone, and have been found at Anghelu Rujiu, Porto Ferro and else-where. They are similar to figures of the Mother Goddess discovered in the Cyclades with accentuated vertical rhythms, abrupt lines and decisive planes, which combine imported figurative traits with others that are more or less autonomous. The result is that the emphasis on the sexual characteristics usually found in figurines of this kind is less marked. 'Figurines exuding motherliness, as well as carved bulls' heads' write Lilliu, 'are always found together in burial-grounds. They reveal not only a mode of thought peculiar to a religion in which the mother-figure and matriarchy are predominant, but also the economic and agricultural stage of development . . . The destiny of plants and human beings pursues its course through the birth-death-rebirth cycle; the earth-goddess, envisaged as a mother, erotic in her nudity and joined to her mate Taurus (who is also symbolic of sexual potency in males), thus becomes the goddess of death the creatrix.'

A wide interval, lasting as much as half a millennium, separates sculpture in Sardinia during the Copper Age from the earliest Nuraghic bronze figurines. The task of ascribing an exact date to the period in which these bronze figurines were produced is not easy; and the views of archaeologists differ considerably. Some place them as early as the 16th century BC, others suggest a date a little before the Roman conquest.

These bronze figurines are a fine example of the extent to which a minor statue-making art can express the everyday life, beliefs, social structure, customs and myths of an age. The various social classes and trades are represented by figurines ranging from men-at-arms and mantled priestesses (in whom was invested the matriarchal authority already mentioned) to the humble, girdled women of the people, the musicians who played at ritual festivities, and gesticulating dancers. Chiefs and warriors too, despite their solemn, aristocratic air, were an integral part of daily life. Nor should magic symbols and swords surmounted with deer be overlooked; they are of distant Paleolithic origin and obscure in meaning, but are undoubtedly connected with the exorcisms which played a great part in religious observances.

These figurines convey an idea of the everyday existence of early Sardinian society – its haughty isolation, severity, vigour and rigid simplicity. It has rightly been observed that they attempt to solemnise the activity of a farming civilisation imbued with magical and totemistic attitudes; and that they are also suggestive of matriarchal rule. The idea of man as the measure of all things, with art as the expression of thought and culture, is quite remote from these works. It must be stressed again that art as an independent activity occurs only in far more sophisticated cultures; the fact that such a notion was obviously never entertained by Sardinian sculptors is a further demonstration of the islanders' primitive character.

At this juncture it must inevitably be asked just how this sculpture began. Its occurrence is all the more surprising in that no traces of a general figurative culture are to be found in the island, which is devoid of the major traditions in sculpture and painting that are present in other early cultures. As a rule, archaeologists seek its origins outside Sardinia, above all in the Eastern Mediterranean; but this is not an entirely satisfactory explanation of all its formal peculiarities. It seems necessary to posit a connection with the figurines carved locally in basalt, limestone and marble during the Copper Age, despite the interval of nearly half a millennium separating them from the earliest Nuraghic bronze figurines. It is on the basis of this tenacious archaic tradition, and following cautious changes in form, that Nuraghic bronze figurines eventually emerge. Their external origin in the Cyclades is on this view so indirect as to be less important than the creative contribution made by the local culture. Nuraghic figurines belong to an art whose practitioners were searching for an order all their own, a process spread over a wide span of time; and, what is more, this took place with few repetitions or clichés. However, the four hundred or so bronze figurines discovered to date must also be seen as a part of a geometric culture that flourished in the Mediterranean for a millennium at the end of the prehistoric age.

The sense of line, the use of planes, the rhythm of form and rigorous moulding all spring from a deep understanding of the value of mass in primary figures – the rectangle, hexagon, trapezium and rhomboid – on which the bronze figurines are entirely based. Those revealing greater force of expression have a vitality and inventiveness which leads one to believe that they are the work of authentic artists. Examples of these are the *Tribal Chief*, the *Mother of the Slain Man* and the *Mantled Priestess;* in these, geometrical planes are effectively used for stylistic value. It must be stressed that the utilisation of geometry in ancient Sardinia is in no way related to the Classical order, but on the contrary corresponds more closely to the almost abstract rhythms found in Germanic art, of the type that were to reappear in the wake of the Scythians, Sarmatians and Scandinavians during the decline of the Roman Empire. Modern interest in Nuraghic sculpture and other forms of primitive art may be partly ascribed to the anti-Classical spirit of the age in which we live.

The most homogeneous group of bronze figurines, and perhaps the finest discovered so far, come from the region of Uta, near Cagliari. They have been made with a subtle feeling for proportions that is emphasised by the restrained accentuation of ascending rhythms in both the slender torsos and the graceful, slightly elongated necks. They also display a sense of geometry which, as has already been pointed out, is clearly linked with the style of Copper Age Sardinian figurines; this is particularly appropriate to the aloof detachment of the figures, which is intended to create an impression of seriousness removed from the everyday. The *Tribal Chief* (shown with his right arm raised), the *Slinger* and even the *Archer with Drawn Bow* may be taken as examples, since both the figures and the values they symbolise are represented with the utmost formal discipline. A very different feeling – for man as a reality in an individual condition – is manifest elsewhere, for example in the *Serri Chief*. Similarly, in the *Mother of the Slain Man* abstract rigour is combined with a powerfully expressive rendering of the event. Nonetheless the search for forms of expression is essentially one concerning volume and structure, and is directed towards a characteristically primitive relationship between full and empty spaces.

A second group of figurines, from Abini (near Nuoro), differ considerably from those found at Uta. They are less formal and display an insistence on using established decorative solutions. A taste for over-stylised ornamentation is combined with a desire for pictorial effects (even of light and shadow) and a vivid expressionism that entails the abandonment of geometrical elements. This recalls the Phoenicians, the Carthaginians or even the Etruscans, in that these figurines are suggestive of a more direct Eastern influence, however indistinct the relationship. The best of these figurines were produced by artists fully capable of skilfully blending volume and design, form and taste, as in the *Sardinian Soldier-of-Fortune* and the *Hero with Two Shields*.

Alongside these two main tendencies may be placed the bronze figurines found at Barbagia, which have a distinct physiognomy of their own. They are pervaded by an anti-geometrical feeling for natural reality, and are at once more free and more 'popular' in style. This plebeian or everyday quality is the first thing one notices; but despite this interesting characteristic they are as a whole inferior to the other two groups. In brief, they are evidently the products of a less refined culture, closed to outside influences and therefore drawing on its own resources; the forms are soft and somewhat unambitious, reflecting a kind of impressionistic vision of everyday life.

To sum up, Nuraghic sculpture developed in three different directions; recent studies suggest that they were contemporaneous, and corresponded with three different forms of culture flourishing in the island.

A further marginal tendency which must not be overlooked are the small animal figures found at Sta Vittoria di Serri in central Sardinia. Equally remote from the geometric culture of Uta and the realistic and 'popular' work of Barbagia, these bronze animal figurines are attributed to a later age, perhaps between the 4th and 3rd centuries BC, when the direct influence of the Classical cultures flourishing on the mainland of Italy must have been felt. In them a symbolic freshness, a free and dynamic rhythm, and harmony in the relationship between line, light and form are exploited to the full. They, and the more important and numerous figurines discovered at Uta, Abini and Barbagia, demonstrate that the early Sardinians evolved a culture whose degree of accomplishment was considerable; a culture of greater interest than any other in the Western Mediterranean.

SOUTHERN AND EASTERN ITALY AND SICILY

The picture is very different when we pass from Sardinia to Sicily and southern Italy. Any development of note during the Bronze and early Iron Age was of short duration, and involved the manufacture and decoration of pottery rather than sculpture. The reason for this is that, as early as the 8th century BC, both the Chalcidians and the Corinthians had landed in Sicily; they brought with them a wholly revolutionary culture that was to make itself felt on the still primitive local population. Even before the Chalcidians and Corinthians, Sicily had been visited by sailors and merchants from the Levant. Phoenicians and Greeks had probably called at the island occasionally from the earliest times, and later they increased their visits, competing with each other to supply the islanders with metal ores (which were lacking in Sicily) in exchange for agricultural products. For five or six centuries before the Greek hegemony and Roman conquest, therefore, the development of Sicilian and southern Italian cultures varied according to the nature of their relations with foreign cultures.

Western Sicily was inhabited by the Sicans, the eastern end of the island by the Sicels. Both were farming peoples who had settled in the interior of the island, choosing good defensive sites for their villages, and later spreading towards the last line of hills overlooking the sea. Thucydides (5th century BC) wrote that the Sicans were the earliest inhabitants of the island and were perhaps of Spanish origin; and it is thought that during the 11th century BC, the Sicels came to Sicily from southern Italy, where there are traces of their existence. The way of life of both Sicans and Sicels had already been influenced to a large extent by foreign cultures, mainly those of Mycenae and the Near East; almost certain proof of this is the *tholos* at St'Angelo Muxaro, near Agrigento, which dates from the 10th century BC.

The Bronze Age left its greatest mark in the eastern end of the island inhabited by the Sicels, where contact with the rest of the Mediterranean world was established earlier and more easily than elsewhere in Sicily.

The civilisation that evolved at Pantalica, in the Anapo Valley, was perhaps the most complete of all Sicilian cultures. It was a rustic culture whose development was very slow. Artistic objects were almost completely absent; the highlights of this culture are the numerous products of craftsmen, who displayed considerable refinement. Among the finds are pieces of shiny red pottery, heart-shaped amphorae, violin-bow fibulae, and swords and knives with sickle-shaped blades, all of which closely resemble finds from Mycenae. Then, with the advent of the Iron Age, appear villages of round or square huts and burial-grounds with oven-shaped tombs hewn in the rock. Although progress was made and there were improvements in everyday life, standards tended to deteriorate. Craftsmen were apparently no longer guided by tradition, so that the standard of their products steadily declined; and there was a gradually increasing dependence on foreign ideas and styles. In pottery the process of decline is more marked, since both moulding and decoration are poor in quality.

The crisis in aesthetic values and techniques was to come to a head in the 8th century BC. The origin and cause of this crisis are still somewhat obscure, though the rapid and incoherent process of Hellenisation was probably to blame. After all, the impact of the arrival *en masse* of a people with a superior civilisation is overwhelming; and the temptation to copy its products and methods is almost irresitible. It was the greater in this case because Greek penetration into Sicily brought far-reaching social upheavals: the rich middle class of immigrants seized land belonging to the islanders, who in many parts of Sicily (Syracuse, for example) were reduced to a state not much better than that of helots.

The colonisation of eastern Sicily by the Greeks was cautious at first. To begin with, they made small settlements and farmed on a small scale; then they suddenly moved into positions of authority, taking over the administration of farms and estates, of which they became the lords and masters once the unfortunate owners had been ousted. The Greeks' next step was to build cities resembling those of Hellas, and to constitute free and independent states. It was not long before the greater part of Sicily fell under a Greek hegemony stretching from the Ionian Sea to Selinunte and Imera – beyond which lay the region dominated by the Phoenician merchant venturers. The Phoenicians administered their territory from Solunto, Mozia and Panormo. The whole area under Phoenician jurisdiction remained closed to Greek penetration; and even more stringently so after the Carthaginians replaced the Phoenicians.

Thus from the 7th century BC, Sicily was divided between Greeks and Phoenicians, and was accordingly forced to bear the consequences of continued conflict, dictatorships and rivalry among cities.

The earliest evidence of Sicel art dates from the end of the 8th or the beginning of the 7th century BC. Before this there were no established art forms in the island; only inferior local craftsmanship. The advent of the Greeks, and the introduction of anthropomorphic gods, appears to have injected a liberating energy into the islanders. They were furnished with the new ideas and a vast range of Hellenic patterns – all of which were indispensable if figurative art forms were to be created in the island. The whole of Sicilian society was to change under the impact of Greek influence. Life on the island became entirely urbanised, and cities were surrounded by massive walls built to defend the citizens from attack. No sooner had a new colony been founded than either an altar or a temple was consecrated to its tutelary deity; and, so that it should be worthy of him, it was furnished with a statue of the god, appropriate votive casks, clay or marble ornaments, and relief carvings of mythological exploits. Town-planning, civil and military architecture, and sculpture were introduced.

The ranks of imported Greek artists were soon swelled by others born in the island, and Siceliot art forms gradually developed. The first attempts at sculpture can be seen in the series of earliest metopes at Selinunte (three small ones representing the *Rape of Europa,* the *Sphinx* and a group comprising *Latona, Apollo and Artemis*). Outwardly the metopes are Greek, though their local execution is revealed by a certain rigidity of form which indicates that the sculptors who carved them were working according to hurriedly assimilated alien models, in this instance Dorian. In view of this, it is surprising that during this early phase figurines in Sicily and southern Italy already displayed distinct Western characteristics, albeit manifested within the framework of Greek art. The artistic relationship between Greece and Sicily did not develop in one direction alone.

Most minor sculpture was in bronze, and was for the most part still an applied art, intended to embellish other objects. Handles and mirror-supports, decorated with gods, heroes and animals, were made in large quantities. Here, too, local craftsmen worked mainly in the style of the earliest Dorian settlers. However, it was not long before Ionian, Attic and even Rhodian motifs were introduced into Dorian patterns, softening their extreme severity. These handles and mirror-supports were unpretentious works of a certain merit, and were later to influence modern taste.

Minor art in Sicily, when it is not merely the commercialised, vulgarised and ponderous offshoot of Greek colonial art, is almost always enlivened by a touch of the ingenuousness and freshness now valued so much. A considerable number of bronze objects made by Sicilian craftsmen from the 7th century BC onwards have these characteristics; other, similar objects – Greek-made or passive adaptations of Greek designs – are without them.

The same applies to numerous small clay busts used

in the worship of Demeter and Persephone, which began to be produced in large quantities towards the middle of the 5th century BC. At this time Attic taste prevailed in Sicily; it was later to give rise to the highest and most original forms of sculpture in the island. Graceful moulding embodying an attempt to convey essentials only, imaginative dash and restrained use of detail and ornament, indicate a tendency to cling to ancient traditions; this explains the innate modesty that characterised the work of craftsmen in Syracuse, Gela and Selinunte, whose artistic ideas were typically Sicilian. In short, this movement was by no means a barren return to the past, but rather a legitimate, spontaneous survival of essential forms that injected life into the entire production of objects for everyday use. Yet the entire range of these objects – whether for religious reasons or domestic purposes or personal adornment – scrupulously reflects the tastes, manners and fashions of refined Sicilian society, and for luxury and art following the defeat of the Carthaginians at Imera: a state of grace that was to last from the 6th to the 4th century BC. But the refinement that characterised sculpture at this time was later to prove its undoing, for it was not long before mannerism suffocated the vitality of the popular tradition, as well as the freshness and originality of design. Although local craftsmen worked to Greek designs, during the reign of Hiero II in the 3rd century BC, they allowed themselves to be influenced by ponderous Alexandrian tendencies. By this time, profane themes had prevailed and the main centre of production had moved to Centuripe on the slopes of Mount Etna. The vibrating, sensuous terracotta figurines made there are splendid examples of exuberant Hellenism. In the late 3rd century the Romans conquered Sicily, and a new phase began in the history of the island.

The vicissitudes of the various peoples in southern Italy followed much the same pattern; and, as in Sicily, the early appearance of Greek settlers had an important influence on cultural development. But the course of events was by no means entirely the same. To begin with, there was no Greek hegemony in southern Italy, and still less a stimulus of the kind that forced Sicilians to unite against invasion by the Carthaginians. Moreover, rivalries soon flared up between the numerous Greek colonies scattered along the coastline of southern Italy (Croton and Sybaris are examples), and the process of democracy at work in many southern cities weakened the traditions of Dorian conservatism in 'Magna Graecia' and loosened ties with Greece.

It is interesting to note that the 'native' inhabitants

1. Palaeolithic art. Aurignacian-Perigordian period. *The Venus of Savignano sul Panaro*. Museo Pigorini, Rome.

2. Palaeolithic art. Aurignacian-Perigordian period. *The Venus of Chiozza*. Galleria Fontanesi, Reggio Emilia.

3. Palaeolithic art. Aurignacian-Perigordian period. *The Venus of the Balzi Rossi Caves.* Musée des Antiquités Nationales, St Germain-en-Laye.

4. Neolithic art. Small idol. Museo Archeologico Ligure,
Genoa.

5. Bronze Age art. Stone door from a rock tomb in the
necropolis at Castelluccio, near Noto. Museo Archeologico
Nazionale, Syracuse.

6. Bronze Age art. Small bone idol found in the necropolis at Castelluccio, near Noto. Museo Archeologico Nazionale, Syracuse.

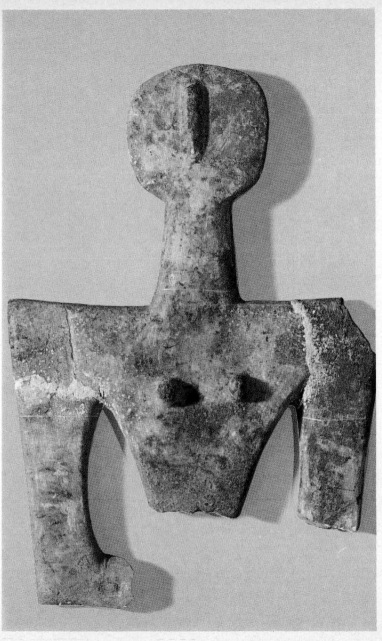

7. Copper Age Sardinian art. Marble figurine found at Porto Ferro. Museo Archeologico Nazionale, Cagliari.

8. Early Sardinian art. *Mater Mediterranea*. Museo
Archeologico Nazionale, Cagliari.

9. Nuraghic art. *Tribal Chief.* Museo Archeologico Nazionale, Cagliari.

10. Nuraghic art. *Slinger.* Museo Archeologico Nazionale, Cagliari.

11. Nuraghic art. *Wrestlers.* Museo Archeologico Nazionale, Cagliari.

12. Nuraghic art. *Archer with Drawn Bow.* Museo
Archeologico Nazionale, Cagliari.

13. Nuraghic art. *Mother of the Slain Man.* Museo
Archeologico Nazionale, Cagliari.

15. Nuraghic art. *Man with Short Beard.* Museo Archeologico
Nazionale, Cagliari.

16. Nuraghic art. *Hero with Four Eyes and Four Arms.* Museo Archeologico Nazionale, Cagliari.

of southern Italy were already becoming involved in local politics as well as in social and cultural activities. Despite this, ancient, obscure traditions persisted; traditions that can only be generally defined as belonging to the Mediterranean megalithic culture. Artists and craftsmen from Apulia, Calabria, Lucania and Campania, though influenced by Greek styles, expressed a spirit all their own in their work – to such an extent that art in the whole of the region essentially constitutes an Italiot interpretation of Greek art. This is much more the case in southern Italy than in Sicily.

Traces have been found in Apulia of a civilisation whose origin is undoubtedly local and whose artistic merits must not be overlooked. It dates from before the time of the Greek settlements in the area and is attributed to the Messapians and Iapygians; if Polybius is to be believed (and admittedly he is not always reliable), they were anything but barbarians. This is supported by the marvellous pottery they produced; the geometrical patterns with which it is decorated reveal the good taste and vivid imagination of its makers. Further evidence in support of Polybius' statement is embodied in the figurative ornamentation and graceful lines of the *trozzella* (a terracotta vase with 'stalks' protruding from the neck); and, last but not least, in the various finds of jewellery (amber or glass paste) and bronze and clay amulets – all of which are to some extent offshoots of Eastern culture.

In Apulia, as elsewhere, burial-grounds supply valuable information about primitive man's history, habits and tastes, both before and after the advent of the Greeks. Inhumation rites predominated throughout southern Italy. The burial-grounds, with their oven-shaped tombs and the funerary ware found in them, supply evidence of a tenacious attachment to the earliest local traditions. The Iapygian burial-grounds discovered at Cannae, Arpi, Canosa, Pizzone di Taranto, Cellino san Marco and Gioia del Colle reveal a common religious outlook that had spread from the Ionian Sea to the northern boundaries of the region as early as the New Stone Age. It appears that many of its characteristics at first resembled aspects of Apenninic civilisation. A visit to the archaeological site at the Scoglio del Tonno, not far from Taranto, provides striking proof of this. It was at first thought that the village unearthed there was a *terramara* settlement of Indo-Germanic origin, though archaeologists now incline to the view that its origin is Apenninic. The village consisted of rectangular huts, and stands on a site in which three distinct strata were brought to light. A few traces of Neolithic civilisation were found in the lowest stratum. The middle stratum contained earthenware of the black Etruscan *bucchero* type, trinklets, arms, axes and scrapers whose characteristics are Apenninic. Finally, much geometrically decorated pottery of Apulian, Mycenaean and early Corinthian origin was found in the top layer. Digging revealed similar strata underlying settlements at Porto Perone (near Leporano) and at Torre Castelluccio. The inhabitants of Torre Castelluccio were probably of Messapic stock. The traditional pottery designs produced by the Messapians are Apenninic verging on the prehistoric, and were used for a greater length of time than elsewhere.

In the earliest times there was no painting and sculpture in Apulia that can be called art. The Greek settlers were undoubtedly a decisive factor in ending this state of affairs; yet it was not long before local craftsmen, who had at first merely imitated Greek models or at least been guided by Greek principles, created works with an unmistakably indigenous, realistic touch. The earliest experiments in vase and mural painting were made in Apulia between the 6th and 5th centuries BC. They had been preceded by a sculpture production comprising both large statues and figurines. The figurines outnumber the large statues, and are in most cases enlivened by an unmistakably Italiot synthetic realism. Nevertheless, minor art in Apulia was not made for utilitarian purposes, or to decorate household objects – an indication of the influence of the Greeks' lofty view of the function of art. Sculptors usually moulded their figurines in clay, which was then baked, covered with a thin layer of lime and painted in bright colours, in a manner that is both unpretentious and pleasing to the eye.

Minor sculpture in Apulia was in the main inspired by religious piety. Sculptors therefore copied down to the last detail the statues of the gods most worshipped in the large temples scattered throughout the region. Among these were the temple at Locri, the temple of Hera at Lacinium, near Croton (dedicated to the cult of Persephone), and the stately temple at Metapontum. Votive and propitiatory figurines were produced in large quantities, and despite a certain fixedness of manner and a conventional expressiveness, local sculptors at times succeed in giving them a a distinctive personal character. Furthermore, their technique is of a refinement that is reminiscent of the engraver's art.

Following Greek domination of the region, figurines of a secular nature were in due course produced on a large scale, and soon surpassed votive figurines as regards both quality and quantity. The rich, worldly society of the south displayed a preference for frivolous though fine terracotta figurines; the National Archaeological Museum at Taranto houses a large collection. This art flourished for several centuries, from about the 6th century BC to the Roman conquest of the region. Its creators were indirectly influenced by the various developments (including changes in style) taking place in major southern sculpture; this, though rarer, was certainly more Greek in form.

One of the main centres of production was Taranto, the *ville lumière* of Magna Graecia. Vast quantites of terracotta figurines, both sacred and profane, have been unearthed here. Carved in full, high or low relief, they reflect the life of Italo-Greek society against a background of luxurious, somewhat melancholy sensuality. It was a society steadily becoming wealthier, more elegant and more pleasure-loving. The range of figurines is indeed wide: statuettes of women with graceful, supple figures, nude or semi-nude; standing or seated gods and goddesses (most commonly Apollo, Demeter and Artemis) with detached and somewhat derisive expressions; athletes and heroes, the popular 'stars' of the age; the satyrs of a disturbingly human aspect.

Yet all was not luxury and ease. The darker side of life finds expression in the grotesque shapes of wretches whose existence was misery; in hunched-up acrobats and buffoons and actors with painted faces. In moulding these figurines, Apulian craftsmen blended the grotesque with satire, tenderness, wit and drama.

The height of realism appears to have been attained by the Daunians, a people who were staunch traditionalists and of whom little is known. The legs, feet, hands, breasts, phalli and small masks of their figurines of children suffice to prove their realism: the limbs are carved with the cold precision of the dissector despite the fact that they are ostensibly votive offerings.

The best examples of this whole wealth of minor sculpture, in which good taste – however humble and rustic – predominates, are undoubtedly the *pinakes,* votive tablets carved in low relief; they throw considerable light on the cult of Castor and Pollux, probably introduced from Sparta at a relatively late date between the 4th and 2nd centuries. Mention must also be made of the *pinakes* found at Locri Epizephyrii in Lucania; they date from the 5th century BC, and are dedicated to the goddess Persephone. Although the refinement of the *pinakes* is indeed singular, even as regards figurative effects, both form and finish are of inferior quality.

Whereas finds of *pinakes* are abundant, few bronze figurines have so far been discovered. Unlike their terracotta counterparts, such figurines were mainly used as in Sicily – to embellish household objects, including vases, candle-holders, arms and sundry instruments. Among the best examples as regards quality of design is the *Banqueter*, which dates from the 6th century BC, and was found at Ruvo; it is now at the British Museum. Curiously enough, both subject and mode of expression closely resemble those of Etruscan funerary figurines. There are also the shoulder-pieces of breastplates discovered at Taranto, which carry lions' heads and scenes of fighting between Greek warriors and Amazons; and the decorative reliefs of plants and animals, used to adorn the feet and heads of beds and couches, and later very popular with wealthy Romans. Other important centres producing figurines in southern Magna Graecia were Reggio and Locri. Apart from the *pinakes* of Locri, there are the numerous figurines of enthroned goddesses found at Reggio. The best of them date from the 6th century BC; and a strong Ionian influence is discernible in them.

Large quantities of votive terracotta figurines were also discovered at the Locrian colony of Medma, on the Tyrrhenian coast. They date from the 5th century

BC, and were used in the cult of Demeter and Cora. The physical traits, attire and decoration of these female figurines are so similar that it seems likely that they were inspired by a particular female type found throughout the region; their coarse, florid good looks are in violent contrast with the graceful features of the figurines from Locri.

North of this region lies Campania. Although Etruscan traces have been discovered in the burial-grounds at Cumae, Capua and Nola, Greek civilisation left a deep imprint on local culture. An indigenous civilisation had existed since the Old and New Stone Ages, but no great schools of art and craftsmanship flourished in the region; it merely produced simple pottery decorated with geometrical motifs of a kind used throughout southern Italy for centuries.

The most important cities on the coastline of Campania were founded by the Greeks, who were engaged in a struggle to hold back the Etruscans pressing on them from the hinterland. From the 6th century BC, abstract ideas began to be given figurative expression in these cities, as vase painting and sculpture gradually developed. Vast numbers of figurines have come to light, especially figurines in clay used for religious purposes; that they served this end is indicative of the southern peoples' religious fervour at this period.

The whole range of figurines is better described as 'artistic craftwork' than as an art form proper; here too it was Italiot in character and closely linked with the figurines already mentioned.

In and around Paestum alone, thousands of votive figurines have been discovered dedicated to Demeter, the goddess of fertility; they express popular local sentiment and are realistically if crudely rendered in terracotta. Some represent uteri and babes in swaddling clothes; others are somewhat unusual in that they represent the female genital organs below enormous swollen bellies. They were clearly turned out by the thousand to satisfy the religious and propitiatory needs of the people, fulfilling much the same purpose as 'holy pictures' or the small figures of saints we see painted on postcards today.

The terracotta figurines dedicated to Hera are very different. The best of them have been found in the sacrificial fonts of the temple at the mouth of the River Sele, and exhibit a development of taste and craftsmanship spanning three centuries. Among them are a skilfully carved figurine dating from the 7th century BC; a figurine of the 5th century BC (plate 27) which, though archaic in form, is mature in taste, representing a goddess enthroned who holds a sacred pomegranate in her right hand; and finally the later representations of Hera Ilithyia (for example plate 28), nude, kneeling, with a winged cupid over either shoulder – by now transformed into a goddess of love. Many of these figurines are enlivened by an almost pictorial contrast of light and shadow playing over their planes.

Other Campania figurines represent the Mother Goddess, seated and suckling her babe – that is, a precursor of the Christian Madonna and Child, though in this instance connected with the cult of Hera of Argos. Still other figurines represent the goddess Minerva, to whom the temple normally bearing the name of Demeter or Ceres must have in fact been dedicated.

On the east coast of central Italy were Samnium and Picenum, which were in a strange position between the 8th and 5th centuries BC, since they were situated in a no-man's land between cultures. The region lay outside the confines of Magna Graecia, while to the west were the various 'Apenninic' cultures. Commercial and artistic exchanges with the 'Eastern' culture of Latium were frequent and lively – a process greatly facilitated by the easy passage through the mountain passes. Although these influences undoubtedly contributed to the formation of the local culture, it never really transcended its provincialism.

Greek influence is also manifest, as a result of direct contact through the centres of commerce at Ancona and Numana, or else indirectly through the Campanians, Daunians and Lucanians.

Despite these conflicting tensions, the civilisation of Picene and Samnite was prevalently Apenninic in character, and remained so for centuries. The Picenes and Samnites, traditionally warriors and peasants, were of Sabellic stock; they adhered to inhumation rites and were not averse to indulging in small, refined pleasures, in this world and the next. The objects in amber and bronze with which they adorned themselves, their elaborate, fanciful jewellery and fine armour, are indicative of their tastes, which are all particularly refined. The refining influence was perhaps their familiarity with the jewellery and gold work of Anatolian, Mycenaean, Egyptian and Assyrian origin imported by the Phoenicians in about the 7th century BC; and also the Latian fashion for jewellery and gold of 'Eastern' design.

That the earliest examples of an indisputably Italic school of sculpture originated from Picenum and Samnium is still more surprising; and as such indicates that a Sabellic 'movement' of representational art did once exist. Proof of this are the carved head of a warrior discovered at Numana and now in the

Ancona Museum; the statue of a warrior found at Capestrano, admirably designed and skilfully moulded; and the expressive bronze figurine of a Samnite warrior now in the Louvre, Paris. The three figurines, neither abstract nor naturalistic, belong to an entirely separate, somewhat mysterious provincial school which evidently reached complete maturity.

THE APENNINES AND THE PO VALLEY

Whereas Greek and Eastern influence on art in Sicily and southern Italy were felt at an early stage, and central Italy gradually advanced in the shadow of a dawning Etruscan civilisation, the Po Valley culture – especially in the region north of the river – was extremely backward. This retardation between the 10th and 5th centuries BC, is revealed by the fact that iron was little used, preference still being given to bronze.

Three ethnic and cultural groups dating from the dawn of history have come to light in northern Italy. The first, the culture of Golasecca, is named after the village on the River Ticino where it originated. Its centre was Lombardy and Piedmont, though its influence was also felt in Liguria. The second, the culture of Este, occupied what is now Venetia. Finally, Villanovan culture spread from Romagna to central Italy along the right bank of the River Tiber. The cultures of Golasecca and Este weathered the Gallic invasion in the 5th century BC, and lingered on till the Roman conquest; whereas Villanovan culture was eventually absorbed by Etruscan civilisation, first in the north, then in the south.

Although the three cultures were somewhat rough and rustic, they undertook cultural exchanges with their neighbours north of the Alps, and were not without a significance peculiarly their own.

As is the case almost throughout Italy, burial-grounds in the Po Valley are very informative about the primitive peoples who inhabited the region. Here the dead were cremated. The origin of this custom dated from at least the time of the *terramara* settlements, and led to the development of a type of pottery whose function was to contain the charred bones of the departed. The burial-grounds were virtual storehouses of urns, usually furnished with small quantities of mediocre funerary ware. Most of the clay cinerary urns unearthed in the region are biconical in shape, flattened so as to form a double-convex outline, while the truncated cones are joined at the base. The urns are decorated with geometrical motifs engraved in the wet clay before baking; they vary from 'wolf's-teeth' designs and bands to horizontal, vertical and wavy lines. At a later date, *situla*-shaped, globe-shaped and oval urns, painted black or brown, began to be made. A long period was to pass before these somewhat crude urns were superseded by more slender vessels decorated with less conventional motifs.

Apart from a few prehistoric tombs, the best finds of the Golasecca culture were made at Ca' Morta, situated not far from Como, between Rebbio, Breccia and Grandate. The numerous finds give a fairly good idea of the period between the end of the Bronze Age and the beginning of Roman influence on local culture.

Tombs excepted, this culture evolved slowly and was particularly backward at the westward end of the region. The few traces of artistic production, as well as the cinerary urns, small quantities of funerary ware, and the various ornamental objects made of glass paste, bronze or amber, all reveal a marked crudeness of taste and technique. Incidentally, the amber used for making ornamental objects was imported from north of the Alps; magic powers were ascribed to it in both northern and southern Italy. To these objects must be added the small finds of bird-shaped terracotta vases; bronze discs with geometrical motifs in relief; *situlae* decorated with animals in relief in designs curiously reminiscent of Eastern and Celtic art; a bowl decorated with imaginary animals (found at Castelletto Ticino, where traces of Gallic culture have come to light); and finally the slightly more realistic representations of dogs, swans and plants, in which the strong influence of Este appears. These finds are only rarely the fruit of creative imagination on the part of early Lombard craftsmen; and as such are of little interest or importance in the history of art.

Rock engravings are scattered throughout the region. It must be stressed that they are essentially a continuation of those executed in the Old Stone Age, though cruder and more summary than their predecessors; a clear demonstration that the people of the Golasecca culture were extremely unadventurous and chary of creating new art forms. Rather than invent new art forms or adapt those of other cultures, the Lombard peasantry apparently found it easier to import pottery and other household objects directly from Venetia and Etruria in exchange for agricultural products or livestock. Although finds from the burial-ground at S'Bernardino reveal that some progress had been made after the introduction of the potter's wheel, there is little evidence of artistic improvement – and this, despite the fact that there have been tomb finds that date from as late as the Gallic invasion in the 5th century BC. The dearth of original art forms is in fact more acute in the third and last phase of the Golasecca culture, which preceded the Roman conquest of the region.

There is also little evidence that towns and cities were built. The inhabitants, mainly peasants and shepherds, lived in clusters of huts in which there were no meeting-places or other social centres. They must have been very peace-loving, since few arms have been unearthed in the numerous tombs so far discovered.

The picture is very different in the lower or eastern reaches of the Po Valley. Here palaeo-Venetic civilisation – the culture of Este – evolved and flourished from the 9th century BC. This region, like that of the Golasecca culture, abounded in burial-grounds and lacked towns and cities; but the working of metal ores reached an advanced stage of development. The famous bronze *situlae* were being made as early as the 7th century BC; the first prototypes were in all probability imported from Crete or from north of the Alps, as the technique of decorating them in relief would suggest. The fact that the inhabitants were engaged in working metals suggests that they felt a need to express themselves in representational art forms which, beginning with *situlae*, were later to

17. Nuraghic art. *Hero with Two Shields.* Museo Archeologico Nazionale, Cagliari.

19. Siceliot art of the 6th and 5th centuries BC. White terracotta bust of a woman. From Selinunte. Private collection, Milan.

20. Italiot art of the 6th and 5th centuries BC. Clay head of an offerer. Museo Archeologico Nazionale, Naples.

21. Italiot art of the 6th and 5th centuries BC. Clay head of an offerer. Museo Archeologico Nazionale, Naples.

23. Lucanian art of the 6th century BC. *Small Horse.* Museo Archeologico Provinciale, Potenza.

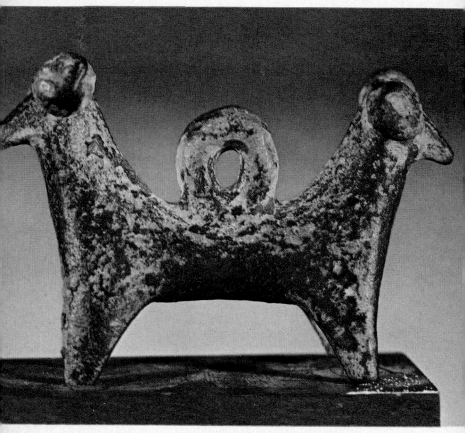

24. Lucanian art of the 6th century BC. Bronze figurine of a double-headed ram. Museo Archeologico Provinciale, Potenza.

25. Lucanian art of the 6th century BC. *Bull.* Museo
Archeologico Provinciale, Potenza.

26. Italiot art of the 6th century BC. *Artemis.* Musée du Louvre, Paris.

27. Campanian art dating from the middle of the 5th century BC. *Hera Enthroned.* Museo Archeologico Nazionale, Paestum.

28. Campanian art of the 3rd century BC. *Hera Ilithyia.* Museo Archeologico Nazionale, Paestum.

29. Apulian art of the 3rd century BC. *Woman with Black and White Robe.* Museo Archeologico Nazionale, Taranto.

30. Apulian art of the 5th century BC. *Jester*. Museo Archeologico Nazionale, Taranto.

31. Locrian art of the 5th century BC. Votive tablet. Museo Nazionale, Reggio Calabria.

34. Picene art of the 6th century BC. *The Warrior of Numana.*
Museo Archeologico delle Marche, Ancona.

35. Golasecca culture. Anthropomorphic clay vase. Museo Archeologico, Como.

36. Palaeo-Venetic art of the 3rd century BC. Bronze figurine of a woman. Museo Nazionale Atestino, Este.

37. Palaeo-Venetic art of the 6th and 5th centuries BC. *The Hercules of Contarina*. Museo Nazionale Atestino, Este.

38. Palaeo-Venetic art of the 3rd century BC. Bronze votive figurine. Museo della Magnifica Comunità Cadorina, Pieve di Cadore.

39. Villanovan art. Terracotta vase. Museo Civico, Bologna.

40. Villanovan art. Receptacle in the form of a bull-shaped wine-skin. Museo Civico, Bologna.

41. Villanovan art. *The Gozzadini Head*. Museo Civico, Bologna.

42. Villanovan art of the 4th century BC. Funerary *stele* discovered near Bologna. Museo Civico, Bologna.

43. Villanovan art of the 5th century BC. Cup. Museo Archeologico Nazionale, Ferrara.

44. Villanovan art of the 6th and 5th centuries BC. Bronze *situla* from the Certosa. Museo Civico, Bológna.

45. Etruscan art of the 7th century BC. Canopic vase in a chair-like receptacle. Museo Archeologico, Florence.

46. Etruscan art of the 6th century BC. Bronze figurine of a woman. Museo Archeologico, Florence.

47. Etruscan art of the 6th century BC. Small cinerary urn with a dancing scene carved in relief. Museo Nazionale Archeologico, Palermo.

48. Etruscan art of the 6th and 5th centuries BC. *Warrior about to throw a spear*. Museo di Villa Giulia, Rome.

find expression in a wide range of household objects, arms included. The movement later spread north of the Po as far as the Danube.

Situlae are the most important products of Venetic culture; from the 5th century BC onwards they were decorated with elegant geometrical motifs or scenes with warriors, lions, sphinxes, centaurs and flowers (for example, the fine Benvenuti *situla*). Although these scenes recall rather similar ones in the Eastern art of two centuries before, they nevertheless have a typically local vivacity and freshness. *Situlae* must certainly have been popular, since they were exported in large quantities both north and south of the Alps. Finds of undoubted Venetic origin have been made in (among other places) Slovenia (for example, the Vace *situla*) and Austria.

Ateste, or Este as it is known today, was the main social, cultural and 'industrial' centre, where bronze was worked on a large scale; and for this reason Este gradually grew in importance over the centuries. Thus Eastern patterns, perhaps imported via the upper Adriatic, eventually evolved into a whirling profusion of curved lines – bizarrely imaginative arabesques tending towards the abstract. Such transformations, in which imported designs undergo radical changes in the hands of artists, indicate an advanced culture; and the resultant works are, in every meaningful sense of the words, original works of art. Furthermore, the works in bronze produced at Este are decidedly anti-Classical. This confirms the vitality of the native culture; and its artistic independence is also shown by the fact that not much Greek pottery has come to light at Este despite the large quantities excavated in the nearby sites at Adria and Spina.

Creative ability is also evident in the bronze figurines used in the worship of Raetia, a benign female deity whose cult flourished from the end of the 4th century BC in a sanctuary not far from the city. The figurines are of men, women, warriors, and matrons with shawls draped over their heads and shoulders in keeping with Venetic custom; they are moulded in lively popular fashion, displaying a slight Gallic influence. As a whole, in form and finish the figurines are on a par with the bronze figurines discovered at Calalzo, Montebelluna and Vicenza; and as such they reveal that attempts were already being made to create plastic art forms in northern Italy. The point is worth making because a major movement in sculpture was wholly lacking in the region throughout the Iron Age.

Villanovan culture gave birth to the earliest forms of representational art in the Po Valley; echoes of

Mediterranean culture are discernible in them. The origin of Villanovan culture is undoubtedly 'Apenninic', in this instance Umbrian; it was imported into the region by migratory peoples who came into Italy from Eastern Europe by way of the Alps and Adriatic, bringing with them the custom of cremating the dead. It is thought that the earliest centres of Villanovan culture were situated in the Apennines between Upper Latium, Umbria and Tuscany. Burial-grounds that date from about the 11th century BC, have been discovered there; they contain funerary ware more advanced than that produced elsewhere.

The region in which Villanovan culture flourished may be divided into two zones lying north and south of what is now called 'the Gothic Line'. Some archaeologists have baptised the culture in the southern zone 'Tarquinese', after Tarquinia. Although its beginnings were quite early, dating from the 11th century BC, it had already been absorbed by Etruscan civilisation three centuries later. The northern zone, styled 'Bolognese' by archaeologists, took longer to develop; and thus its beginnings are dated not earlier than 930 BC. Although it was almost completely free from penetration by other cultures until the 5th century BC, exchanges did take place with centres to the north in Venetia.

It was during the third phase of the northern or Po Valley zone that sculpture began to develop. At first horses' heads and figurines of ducks in clay or bronze were moulded, though they were soon followed by an interesting development in the form of the *stele*, a truly singular offshoot from the prehistoric menhir. Representation in art usually passes by numerous stages from stylised or geometrical motifs to realistic portrayal; so relief carving on *stelae* at first tended to be abstract and eventually became figurative.

Villanovan culture was at its best between the second half of the 8th and the end of the 7th century BC. By this time settlements had grown into towns and cities, the local economy had been transformed from a patriarchal system of administration into one governed by guilds of craftsmen, and the plastic arts, hitherto in embryo, at last came into their own. The creative abilities of Villanovan craftsmen were best expressed in funeral monuments. Among these are a truncated cone-shaped *cippus* (monumental column) surmounted with a human head discovered at S'Giovanni in Persiceto; a rectangular *stele* surmounted with a disc, which is either a symbolic representation of the sun or a schematic rendering of the human body; the Zannoni *stele*, dating from the 6th century BC, which depicts a dead man's journey to the lower regions, and revealing the influence of Mycenaean, and even Syro-Hittite *stelae* mysteriously imported into the Po Valley; and the *stele* discovered at Saletto Bentivoglio which dates from about 500 BC, and is a curious figurative synthesis of Etruscan and Venetic plastic art. Difficult though it appears, it is possible to distinguish between mere passive absorption of a foreign influence and persistent indigenous trends in these *stelae* – apart from anything else, because the indigenous trends are far more comprehensible.

Also of considerable importance in art history, are the Villanovan *situlae* which, in addition to geometrical motifs, are adorned with representations of animals, sphinxes, warriors, and scenes from everyday life. In later bronzeware of the 'Certosa' period, in which Etruscan influence is strong, typically local features are always present: a certain ingenuousness and severity of form and a realistic, almost documentary manner.

Credit is due to the creativity of Villanovan culture, and its ability to absorb foreign forms and decorative motifs, for having provided yet another link in the historical and artistic evolution of whole regions of Italy. For it was Villanovan culture, after it had gradually been absorbed by Etruscan civilisation, (by now fully evolved in south central Etruria), that enabled the latter to have access to the Po Valley.

Moreover, Villanovan culture influenced the Etruscans in the production of pottery. In this respect, Etruscan *bucchero* pottery and canopic vases from Chiusi appear to be direct offshoots from the earliest pottery produced in the Apenninic region.

THE ETRUSCANS

There are three schools of thought regarding the origin of the Etruscans. The first school maintains that they came to Italy by sea from Asia Minor and the Near East; the second that they travelled overland from Central Europe; the third that they had always lived in Italy. For this and many other reasons the Etruscans have always been considered a mysterious people, and have always aroused interest and curiosity in both specialists and laymen.

Ancient authors were equally nonplussed. Herodotus, conforming to a theory put forward by Ionian historians before him, held that the Etruscans originated in Lydia in Asia Minor and later emigrated to Western Europe to escape famine in their own land; and that they were led in their flight by the mythical Tyrrhenus, the son of King Atys of Lydia. On the other hand, Dionysius of Halicarnassus – presumedly a native of Asia Minor – believed that the Etruscans were one of the autochthonous people of Italy. During the 18th century variance of opinion became even more marked; Etruria was rediscovered and an ever widening interest was taken in its antiquities.

But no end of ethnographic, historical and comparative philological research, still less archaeological excavation and countless finds, have been able to solve the problem once and for all. The pre-Hellenic inscriptions on the funerary *stele* found at Kaminia on the island of Lemnos in the Aegean Sea provide some light. The alphabet used in these inscriptions is not Greek and has never been deciphered, though it is very similar to that used by the Etruscans. These inscriptions provide support for the theory of the Etruscans' Near Eastern origins, as does the Eastern element that appears in the greater part of Etruscan art, even at a primitive stage of its development.

For present purposes it is sufficient to record that as early as the 9th century BC, a people known by the name of Rasna or Rasenna inhabited the central and western regions of Italy. Their most striking characteristic was an intense religiosity. They believed that their destinies were guided by supernatural beings that were possessed of a personality but not easily identified; and they therefore took great pains to scrutinise and interpret the various omens portending good or evil. These omens included lightning, the most important manifestation of the great god Tinia; the entrails, especially the liver, of sacrificed animals; and the flight of birds. The complex ritual ceremonies of scrutiny and interpretation were conducted by the priestly class of *haruspices*, who were governed by a rigid code in the performance of their duties. The beliefs of the Rasennae regarding the creation of the universe were very similar to the Biblical account. Their belief in an afterlife had a decidedly pessimistic chant: they held that although the souls of the departed survived death, their well-being was constantly endangered by an army of demons. Among the latter were Charun, the horrific Tuchulcha and the Lasae, whose evil influence could be warded off only by veneration of the dead by the living caring for the tombs of the dead, and the consoling presence in tombs of the objects to which the dead had been most attached during their lives. From this it is clear that the religious beliefs of the Rasennae were in many respects similar to those held in ancient Egypt and Mesopotamia, and contrasted strongly with those of the Greeks, who created deities in their own likeness. A religious life as fervent and articulate as that led by the Rasennae is possible only in a society whose people possess a degree of security and comfort. Certainly in its earliest stages of development, Etruscan civilisation fulfilled both conditions. The fertile plains of ancient Etruria, accessible mountains and rich mineral deposits (especially iron) contributed to make life relatively pleasant and easy for the inhabitants, and also enabled them to enjoy considerable economic independence. Diodorus Siculus justly described Etruria as the 'land of plenty'. Prosperity at home was soon followed by maritime trading and cultural exchanges which enabled Etruria to take her place among the principal Mediterranean civilisations.

The highest and most complex civilisation in Italy before the Romans was thus evolved. That Etruscan civilisation had already developed from a proto-historic stage is clear from its social organisation, and especially the organisation of towns. The Etruscans, like the Sumerians and Babylonians, were a people who managed to combine other-wordly religion with worldly realism. Here too, tombs give a good picture of daily life in Etruria – at least the life of the rich and powerful – immediately after the first, more rustic Villanovan stage. Houses were large and sumptuously furnished with statues, richly decorated pottery, jewellery and trinkets; exquisite toilet articles including finely engraved mirrors and fanciful bird-shaped perfume-holders; braziers and candle-holders ornamented with figurines and geometrical motifs; amphorae, *situlae* and cists. The whole range of bronzes, ivories, alabaster, gold and silverware reveals a markedly Eastern refinement of taste.

The Etruscans were both makers and consumers of art on a large scale. Their art was at one with their religious outlook; the journey to the lower regions made by the souls of the dead quickly found figurative expression in all forms of art. Etruscan civilisation was basically urban: a network of confederated cities forming the state, and these cities were built to a precise plan calculated in accordance with the position of the heavenly bodies. The arched gates leading into the cities were decorated with busts and sacred animal heads. The hub of each city was the temple, raised on a high plinth and adorned with a profusion of splendid, multi-coloured terracotta figures.

Etruscans tombs, whether in the form of a vault or tumulus, are always monumental and call to mind Sardinian and Mycenaean megalithic structures and the large burial-grounds of Asia Minor. Tombs provided the dead with a subterranean home of spacious and luxurious rooms, furnished with couches similar to those they had used when alive; on these they reclined beneath the somewhat enigmatic gazes of young athletes, musicians and banqueters painted on the walls. Within close reach of the couches or hanging from the walls were the dead person's belongings: arms, shields, helms, pottery, wallets and sundry utensils.

Where inhumation rites were used, tombs were constructed like houses; but wherever the dead were cremated, as in the region of Clusium (Chiusi), where Apenninic culture predominated, ashes were preserved in special urns in which both Villanovan and Egyptian influence is evident. To these globe-shaped canopic urns or ossuaries, made of bronze, *bucchero* or terracotta, the Etruscans added a touch peculiarly their own; the covers of the urns were shaped to resemble the features of the dead man or woman. This characteristic is found throughout Etruscan funerary sculpture, and apart from canopic ossuaries embraces the whole range of sarcophagi and small square urns. The purpose of the custom was to hand down 'portraits' of ancestors to their descendants. It was in fact from this purely Etruscan custom that the art of portraiture developed in Italy.

Although it is not easy to distinguish exactly between major and minor art in Etruria (as it is in Greek and other cultures), it may be assumed that minor sculpture dominated the field. There is unfortunately little evidence as to the standing of artists in Etruscan society, or for that matter of the relative evaluations of, say, a large statue carved by a skilled sculptor and a figurine made by a humble craftsman. Inspiration, liveliness, and formal, dramatic effects are certainly not lacking in sculpture of both kinds; but since there were no 'schools' of art, archaeologists are unable to identify individual sculptors (with the exception of the mythical Vulca), though diligent research may lead to sculptures being roughly classified into groups.

It is difficult to ascertain how far the early geometrical abstractionism of Etruscan art is an original discovery and how far it is simply a renewal and continuation of archaic motifs. There are scholars who maintain that Etruscan art was never at any time independent of first Eastern and later Greek influences; but although it has much in common with both, its constant contact with indigenous proto-Italic cultures – in particular those of Latium, Picenum and Villanova – must be taken into account; these contacts were in fact such as to suggest that they played an important part in the formation and evolution of Etruscan art.

It may thus be assumed that Etruscan figurative art had its beginnings in the Iron Age, at the time of the founding of Etruscan cities and the high period of Villanovan culture in the 8th and 7th centuries BC.

Thus on the one hand there are terracotta ware and indigenous bronze figurines, the latter somewhat primitive and schematic, but with broad and protruding facial features which, though crudely shaped, are conceived with vigour. They eventually culminated in the curious anthropomorphous canopic urns mentioned earlier, which originated mainly from Clusium and the region surrounding it. On the other hand we have figurines and small heads made of ivory, bronze tripods, bowls and jewellery – in brief, a profusion of fanciful ornaments comprising dragons, animal heads, plumes, scales and spirals, the products of a whimsical imagination drawing inspiration from Egyptian, Syrian and Mesopotamian models.

The particular style and manner peculiar to the region is evident in even the earliest phase of Etruscan art. If we pick at random from the best bronze figurines found in the Bolognese area – for example the two figurines of devotees on a chest dating from the beginning of the 5th Century BC, discovered at Monteguragazza – we at once notice in the moulding and details of the anatomy the qualities characteristic of the more or less coeval figurines discovered in the coastal regions of Etruria bordering the Tyrrhenian Sea. This common element in Etruscan art became all the more evident after Eastern and later Greek trends had influenced it. The same applied to the Etruscan arts after the influence of Peloponnesian and Cretan sculpture had been felt at the beginning of the 6th century BC.

In about the middle of the 6th century BC, Ionian colonisation (by the Phocaeans in particular) transformed attitudes towards art down the entire length of the Tyrrhenian coast. The innovations introduced by Ionian civilisation were probably congenial to the Etruscans – far more so than the severe, abstract and conventionalised manner of Crete and the Peloponnese. The Ionian preference was for free moulding of figurines, and they tended to transform rigid geometrical patterns into arabesques and delicate linear rhythms; both features must have been sympathetic to Etruscan craftsmen who worked with spontaneity and zest in a manner at once realistic and expressionistic.

From this period, Greek art, imported into the region in the form of pottery later imitated locally, was the predominant force, and in the last decades of the 6th century BC Etruria became one of the regions in which a figurative culture within a framework of Greek archaism was most marked. This applied above all to minor sculpture, whether in clay or bronze, which was produced in large quantities and was certainly the most exuberant in Italy before the founding of Rome. In both the moulding of figurines in high relief and the ornamentation of luxury objects, Etruscan craftsmen had by now achieved considerable stylistic control and refinement of expression. They also displayed a fine sense of formal rhythm and a fluent disposition of lines and planes. The splendid bronze figurines found at Castel S. Mariano are fine examples of the Ionico-Etruscan culture.

The creativity of Ionico-Etruscan culture was destined to be short-lived, for the evolution of Classicism in Greece during the 5th century BC was to change the whole course of art. The Etruscans changed in spite of the fact that they were little addicted to the conceptions of harmonious order and the idealisation of man and his image that were characteristic of Classicism. They were eventually successful in developing their own brand of Classicism, though their art soon became imbued with mannerism, producing a welter of fanciful, dramatic forms tending towards archaism. This is not surprising, since the roots of their mannerism were essentially realistic and anti-Classical, and therefore more in keeping with the Etruscan temperament.

Change nevertheless brought about crisis, for the Etruscans could not ignore the themes and formal values of Classicism. In this period of crisis, their work reveals the inconsistencies characteristic of a period of transition. Examples of such work are the small head of a bald, bearded man, found at Orvieto; and also the figurine (found at Perugia) of a warrior wearing an Attic helmet, his right arm raised in readiness to throw a spear. The warrior is elongated in an almost surrealistic manner typical of many bronze votive figurines.

During this period of confusion Greek models were passively copied on a large scale; local craftsmen were intent on satisfying the needs of a snobbish provincial society anxious to emulate the Greek way of life. Excavation at Spina, the large Etruscan port on the Adriatic, and abundant finds of Attic pottery, are further proof that Greek taste, imported across the Adriatic, was exercising a strong influence on Etruscan art. There was also a direct influence from a number of Greek sculptors who had emigrated to Etruria after the Persian invasion of Greece. Evidence of their presence is given by Pliny, who states in his *Naturalis Historia* that the sculptors Eucheir, Diopos and Eugrammos, and the Corinthian sculptor Demaratos, came to work in Italy; and that Damophilos and Gorgasos went to Rome in 493 BC to decorate the Temple of Ceres.

49. Etruscan art of the 6th and 5th centuries BC. Bronze head of Acheloo. Museo di Villa Giulia, Rome.

50. Etruscan art of the 6th century BC. *Woman Holding a Sucking Pig.* Museo di Villa Giulia, Rome.

51. Etruscan art of the 6th century BC. Antefix in the shape of a Gorgon. Museo di Villa Giulia, Rome.

52. Etruscan art of the 6th century BC. Figurines of a warrior and a woman. Museo Archeologico, Florence.

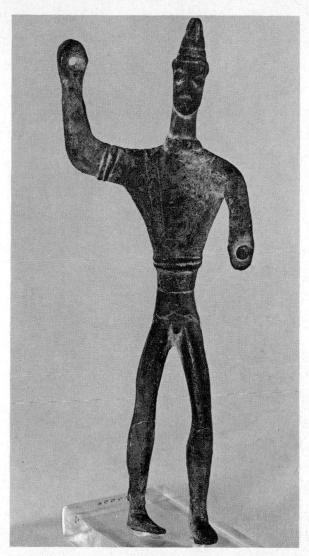

53. Etruscan art of the 6th century BC. *Mars*. Museo di Villa Giulia, Rome.

54. Etruscan art of the 6th century BC. *Aeneas Carrying his Father Anchises on his Shoulders.* Museo di Villa Giulia, Rome.

55. Etruscan art of the 6th and 5th centuries BC. Head of a warrior wearing an Attic helmet. Museo di Villa Giulia, Rome.

56. Etruscan art of the 6th century BC. Jug in the shape of a bull's head. Museo Archeologico, Florence.

57. Etruscan art of the 5th century BC. *Woman and Child.* Museo Archeologico, Florence.

58. Etruscan art of the 5th century BC. *Silenus.* Museo
Archeologico, Florence.

59. Etruscan art of the 4th century BC. Handle of a cist.
Museo di Villa Giulia, Rome.

60. Etruscan art of the 4th and 3rd centuries BC. *Child Playing with a Bird*. Museo di Villa Giulia, Rome.

61. Etruscan art of the 5th-3rd centuries BC. *Head of a smiling child.* Museo di Villa Giulia, Rome.

62. Etruscan art of the 4th and 3rd centuries BC. *Woman with a Child in her Lap and a Cup in her Right Hand.* Museo di Villa Giulia, Rome.

63. Etruscan art of the 4th and 3rd centuries B Two elongated bronze figurines. Museo di Villa Giulia, Rom

64. Etruscan art of the 4th-2nd centuries BC. *Seated Couple.*
Museo di Villa Giulia, Rome.

The output of highly decorated luxury furnishings increased steadily as Etruscan civilisation was far-reaching, all the more so since the star of Rome was now rising quickly. Faced with this situation, the Etruscans became a refined, decadent, conservative society. In this they repeated the reaction of previous cultures confronted with loss of political and military power. To all appearances the Etruscans accepted the role: the existence of the rich became more and more refined and luxurious, and customs and taste became increasingly Hellenised. Sculpture suddenly became elegant and decorative, and artistic representation ended in a welter of imported finesse inspired by Greek and other Classical models. As a result, sculpture diminished in importance as interest became focused on the technical capacities of crafts-men and portrayal of contemporary customs and habits. There are one or two exceptions, however, in several small portrait-busts notable for their ex-pressiveness and sense of realism.

By this time Etruscan representational art had all but declined and was on the point of being swept away for ever by Greek taste. What little remained was to be absorbed by either the nascent Roman civilisa-tion or popular art, which by its very nature discreetly preserves otherwise defunct traditions.

To sum up, Etruscan art first underwent the influence of Villanovan and other Italic cultures from which it acquired expressiveness and realism. These were followed by impulses from Asia Minor, Egypt and Mesopotamia; and finally by the multiple, heady influence of Greek civilisation. All sorts of questions are left open – whether an original Etruscan art ever in truth existed; whether Etruscan culture was of primary or secondary importance; to what extent it really assimilated Greek culture; and so on. But one fact is clear: it is owing to the Etruscans, and their spiritual heirs the Romans, that Greek civilisation, philosophy, ethics and art survived to permeate Western thought. And this, after all, is no small achievement.

LIST OF ILLUSTRATIONS

1. Palaeolithic art, Aurignacian-Perigordian period. *The Venus of Savignano sul Panaro* (22·5 cm). Museo Pigorini, Rome. The protruding breasts and belly indicate ritual and propitiatory functions connected with procreation. This 'Venus' was probably carved from a stone taken from a river-bed.

2. Palaeolithic art, Aurignacian-Perigordian period. *The Venus of Chiozza* (20·5 cm). Galleria Fontanesi, Reggio Emilia. Discovered at Scandiano, in Emilia. The figurine is another striking example of the 'Venuses' carved in sandstone to glorify fertility and womanhood. Throughout Europe — from Russia and Scandinavia to France and the Mediterranean — the aim of Palaeolithic sculpture was to extol the mother-figure: woman as the guardian of life's mysteries.

3. Palaeolithic art, Aurignacian-Perigordian period. *The Venus of the Balzi Rossi Caves* (10 cm). Musée des Antiquités Nationales, St Germain-en-Laye. The over-emphasised breasts, belly and buttocks of this 'Venus' — more pronounced when seen in profile — form an imaginative juxtaposition of geometrical volumes which, though roughly carved, do not lessen the marked anatomical realism characteristic of the whole range of 'fat-rumped' figurines.

4.　Neolithic art. Small idol (4 cm). Museo Archeologico Ligure, Genoa. Traces of a civilisation that had its beginnings in the early part of the Old Stone Age and continued into the Iron Age were discovered in the Grotta delle Arene Candide in Liguria. A piece of pottery decorated with stamped geometrical motifs as well as several stone Venus figurines and small idols were dug out of the stratum dating from the New Stone Age. This is the best example of the small idols discovered.

5.　Bronze Age art. Stone door from a rock tomb in the necropolis at Castelluccio, near Noto. Museo Archeologico Nazionale, Syracuse. One of the most outstanding pieces of Sicilian sculpture at its earliest stage of development. Both Eastern and Western influence is evident in the geometrical motif carved in relief. In all probability the door dates from between the 18th and 15th centuries BC.

6.　Bronze Age art. Small bone idol found in the necropolis at Castelluccio, near Noto. Museo Archeologico Nazionale, Syracuse. The geometrical motifs, engraved or carved in relief, resemble those in numerous artistic objects found in the Peloponnese and on the coast of Asia Minor. It may therefore be assumed that contact was made between Aegean and Sicilian cultures in the course of maritime commerce.

7.   Copper Age Sardinian art. Marble figurine found at Porto Ferro (18 cm). Museo Archeologico Nazionale, Cagliari. Comparable with small figures carved in the Cyclades, the islands in the Aegean to the north of Crete. The severe outline emphasises the two-dimensional planes and angles. The figurine was found near Cagliari.

8.   Early Sardinian art. *Mater Mediterranea* (44 cm). Museo Archeologico Nazionale, Cagliari. The level surfaces of this marble figurine are undoubtedly derived from Cycladic sculpture. It may thus be regarded as a link between Aegean sculpture and the bronze figurines made in Sardinia during the Nuraghic period. The figurine was found at Senorbi, near Cagliari, and embodies the best expressive qualities of Sardinian Copper Age art.

9.   Nuraghic art. *Tribal Chief* (29 cm). Museo Archeologico Nazionale, Cagliari. Structural qualities prevail over all other formal values in this bronze figurine, one of the many belonging to the culture of Uta which have been found at Santa Vittoria di Serri. The various parts of the figurine are all based on the elementary principle of level geometrical surfaces.

10. Nuraghic art. *Slinger* (15 cm). Museo Archeologico Nazionale, Cagliari. This also belongs to the culture of Uta. The moulding is such that a perfect balance is struck between form and matter, while the lines, both curved and straight, give the figure a restrained tautness.

11. Nuraghic art. *Wrestlers* (10 cm). Museo Archeologico Nazionale, Cagliari. The composition — two wrestlers locked in combat — is a fine example of the vitality of Sardinian work; the continuity of lines, though kept in check, creates a splendid spatial effect.

12. Nuraghic art. *Archer with Drawn Bow* (18 cm). Museo Archeologico Nazionale, Cagliari. The gravity and dignity of this figure reflect the approach to life characteristic of Sardinian hierarchical order which, however rude, had great vigour and an evident suspicion of superfluous ornament.

13. Nuraghic art. *Mother of the Slain Man* (10 cm). Museo Archeologico Nazionale, Cagliari. An accomplished and moving work; the sculptor was clearly trying to represent a real – not a merely symbolic or conceptualised – event. The severe lines of the two figures are admirably expressive.

14. Nuraghic art. *Mantled Princess* (18 cm). Museo Archeologico Nazionale, Cagliari. Sardinian civilisation was matriarchal: women were the custodians of all magical and ritual knowledge. This figure of a priestess is pervaded with awe for her sacred function.

15. Nuraghic art. *Man with a Short Beard* (12·5 cm). Museo Archeologico Nazionale, Cagliari. The short beard lends a slightly comical air to the figurine, but as a whole it reflects the hierarchical solemnity of Sardinian civilisation.

16. Nuraghic art. *Hero with Four Eyes and Four Arms* (19 cm). Museo Archeologico Nazionale, Cagliari. The principle underlying sculpture from Uta and Cagliari is strictly geometrical; by contrast, figurines from Abini, near Nuoro, tend to be either decorative or expressionistic, like this one.

17. Nuraghic art. *Hero with Two Shields* (15 cm). Museo Archeologico Nazionale, Cagliari. The sculptor has rendered the *Hero with Two Shields* with a touch of fantasy. It is in all probability an amulet or propitiatory idol.

18. Nuraghic art. *Man Gesticulating* (17·5 cm). Museo Archeologico Nazionale, Cagliari. There are no traces here of the geometrical severity found in figurines from Uta or the decorative touches in those from Abini. This one from Barbagia has a typically lively and plebeian air; the figure gesticulates with all the enthusiasm of his Mediterranean descendents.

19. Siceliot art of the 6th and 5th centuries BC. White terra-cotta bust of a woman (11 cm). From Selinunte. Private collection, Milan. Traces of the archaic traditions of Greek art and sculpture are evident in the details and decoration of this bust, which was used in the worship of Demeter and Persephone. In fact the various forms and styles of minor sculpture are a natural survival of these archaic traditions.

20. Italiot art of the 6th and 5th centuries BC. Clay head of an offerer. Museo Archeologico Nazionale, Naples. This head from Magna Graecia is very similar to those made in Sicily during the same period. It is also a typical example of the popular figurine sculpture that flourished in the Greek colonies scattered along the coast of Italy — a movement more widespread in Italy than in Greece.

21. Italiot art of the 6th and 5th centuries BC. Clay head of an offerer. Museo Archeologico Nazionale, Naples. The head is also a product of the intermingling of Greek and Italic art, as a result of which a more human Italic sculpture inspired by Greek models developed. Local art later developed characteristics peculiarly its own.

22. Campanian art of the 5th century BC. *Seated Woman.* Museo Provinciale Campano, Capua. Discovered in the ruins of an Italic temple at Sta Maria Capua Vetere; the figure is utterly unlike Greek sculpture of the period. The artistic tendencies characteristic of Campanian sculpture are revealed in the anatomical details carved from life.

23. Lucanian art of the 6th century BC. *Small Horse.* Museo Archeologico Provinciale, Potenza. Of great interest for archaeologists are the small bronze animals discovered in Lucania. They were frequently used as personal ornaments, being attached to necklaces or bracelets. The moulding of the horse, reduced to a minimum of detail, is elegantly geometrical.

24. Lucanian art of the 6th century BC. Bronze figurine of a double-headed ram. Museo Archeologico Provinciale, Potenza, Bronze figurines of a double-headed ram, as a rule dating from the 6th century BC, are frequently found in Campania and Lucania. The manner in which the heads and forelegs are joined, and the stylised rather than figurative representation, suggest that they may have been influenced by the geometrical motifs of Greek models. Whatever the influence, their decorative qualities are indeed fine.

25. Lucanian art of the 6th century BC. *Bull.* Museo Archeologico Provinciale, Potenza. Another example of the skill with which Lucanian sculptors moulded animal figurines; this one is even more stylised than those in plates 25 and 26.

26. Italiot art of the 6th century BC. *Artemis.* Musée du Louvre, Paris. Bronze figurines of deities and heroes found in Magna Graecia are decidly inferior to figurines of humans and animals. Yet there are inevitably exceptions to the rule, as is clear from this figurine of Artemis. Its form, tending towards archaism, is indicative of the principles of sculptural style that had become established throughout southern Italy.

27. Campanian art dating from the middle of the 5th century BC. *Hera Enthroned* (50 cm). Museo Archeologico Nazionale, Paestum. Hera, the goddess of fertility, is shown holding a pomegranate in her right hand and wearing the *polos*, a headdress used by several goddesses. She was much venerated in Campania, and her cult later gave rise to the widespread production of religious figurines. The mature archaic style of the figure, somewhat larger than usual, reveals a high standard of craftsmanship which places it in a category apart from similar figurines made locally.

28. Campanian art of the 3rd century BC. *Hera Ilithyia.* Museo Archeologico Nazionale, Paestum. This figurine is one of the finest discovered in the temple of Hera at the mouth of the River Sele. Greek idealisation and a realism peculiar to Italic sculpture merge in this figurine. It is the culmination of a cult that lasted for three centuries during which Hera, formerly the goddess of fertility, was gradually transformed into a goddess of love.

29. Apulian art of the 3rd century BC. *Woman with Black and White Robe.* Museo Archeologico Nazionale, Taranto. The curves of the body and the soft folds of the robes lend an air of grace to the figurine; feminine sensuality and refinement are blended with delicacy and charm.

30. Apulian art of the 5th century BC. *Jester.* Museo Archeologico Nazionale, Taranto. This jester or madcap playing the fool is a good example of Apulian minor sculpture which approaches the grotesque. Here Tarantine craftsmen have skilfully blended caricature with irony.

31. Locrian art of the 5th century BC. Votive tablet. Museo Nazionale, Reggio Calabria. One of the famous *pinakes* found at Locri Epizephyrii; it was used in the cult of Persephone. Although refined Ionian influence is evident in the delicate moulding, the local tendency to adhere closely to an everyday realism is also apparent.

32. Siceliot art of the 2nd century BC. Clay bust of a girl (32 cm). Private collection, Milan. Portrait-busts of this kind, often a part of funerary furnishings, were introduced into Sicily by the Romans, who had in turn copied them from Etruscan models. harmonious blending of the various cultures that met and mixed in the island is apparent in this bust, which was excavated at Scicli.

33. Italic art of the 6th century BC. *The Warrior of Capestrano* (2·09 m). Museo Civico, Chieti. A fine example of ancient Sabellic sculpture, far removed from Greek influence. The work is outstanding above all on account of the severity of form; and the skilful application of geometrical patterns gives the figure an air of restraint and dignity.

34. Picene art of the 6th century BC. *The Warrior of Numana*. Museo Archeologico delle Marche, Ancona. On the east coast of central Italy, Greek influence on the evolution of sculpture was desultory and indirect, and contact with the cultures of the Apennines and Latium gave rise to tensions and a confusion of styles. The head of this warrior is well designed and carved; it is neither naturalistic nor abstract.

35. Golasecca culture. Anthropomorphic clay vase. Museo Archeologico, Como. The artistic production of the Golasecca culture was somewhat limited in quality as well as quantity. This anthropomorphic vase is nevertheless a curious, ingenuous experiment in expression. The moulding in relief betrays traces of Eastern artistic influence, in all probability imported into Italy through the Upper Adriatic by way of Este.

36. Palaeo-Venetic art of the 3rd century BC. Bronze figurine of a woman (10·3 cm). Museo Nazionale Atestino, Este. This votive figurine, discovered in the temple dedicated to the goddess Raetia near Este, is an interesting product of popular art. The style is unpretentious, and the sculptor who moulded it must have been in close touch with everyday life.

37. Palaeo-Venetic art of the 6th and 5th centuries BC. *The Hercules of Contarina* (16 cm). Museo Nazionale Atestino, Este. The figurine is of a deity — in all probability Hercules — shown clutching a fawn in its left hand. The close attention to detail of the bronze — especially the facial features — and the archaic manner in which the beard is shaped suggest that there must be some sort of connection with contemporary Etruscan sculpture.

38. Palaeo-Venetic art of the 3rd century BC. Bronze votive figurine (9.5 cm). Museo della Magnifica Comunità Cadorina, Pieve di Cadore. The facial features of this figurine are undoubtedly of Veneto-Gallic origin. Inscriptions on it are of considerable importance in the study of pre-Roman alphabets; the name of the figurine, and the name of the person who presented it and the dedication are engraved on the back, arms and left leg.

39. Villanovan art. Terracotta vase. Museo Civico, Bologna. The notches cut into the lip of the vase are clearly the work of an unskilled craftsman, whereas the twisted-cord motif reveals some skill and artistic feeling. This motif is quite commonly found in the early stages of Villanovan culture.

40. Villanovan art. Receptacle in the form of a bull-shaped wine-skin (17·7 cm). Museo Civico, Bologna. This bull-shaped receptacle belongs to the third phase of Villanovan culture. The 'Bull' carries a horse and rider on its back. The carefully executed decoration contrasts strongly with the summary modelling.

41. Villanovan art. *The Gozzadini Head* (27·5 cm). Museo Civico, Bologna. The head, attributed to the first half of the 6th century BC is perhaps meant to represent a male sphinx. It is not so much a sculpture in full relief as an odd juxtaposition of perpendicular planes. This is comprehensible in view of the fact that sculpture in the Po Valley was based on geometrical and linear patterns rather than on moulding in full relief.

42. Villanovan art of the 4th Century BC. Funerary *stele* discovered near Bologna. Museo Civico, Bologna. By the 4th Century BC, Etruscan influence on Villanovan sculpture was already strong. Of all forms of sculpture in the Po-Valley region, funerary *stelae* are the most common and by far the most interesting. The carving in relief depicts a dead man's journey to the lower regions — a motif much used in Villanovan funerary sculpture. A foot-soldier and horseman fighting a duel are carved in the bottom panel.

43. Villanovan art of the 5th Century BC. Cup. Museo Archeologico Nazionale, Ferrara. The head of the woman forming the lower part of the cup is moulded with a degree of elegance and accuracy as regards anatomical detail, while the features are enhanced by the striking contrast of black and white. Many cups of this kind, included in collections of sacred and tomb ware, have been found in those regions of Villanovan culture which underwent Etruscan influence.

44. Villanovan art of the 6th and 5th Centuries BC. Bronze *situla* from the Certosa. Museo Civico, Bologna. In the form of a truncated cone with a rounded lip. This *situla* or pail is made of a thin sheet of bronze covered with embossed figures; it is a fine example of the 'Eastern' art which flourished in Venetia and Emilia before the Roman conquest.

45. Etruscan art of the 7th century BC. Canopic vase in a chair-like receptacle (74 cm). Museo Archeologico, Florence. This canopic vase moulded in reddish clay rests on a chair-like receptacle with a curved back. The vase is decorated with holes and stamped geometric motifs. The lid is shaped in the likeness of the dead man whose ashes it once contained. The moulding of the features is stylised and tends towards the abstract, intensifying the expression of solemn detachment.

46. Etruscan art of the 6th century BC. Bronze figurine of a woman (24 cm). Museo Archeologico, Florence. When moulding the figurine the sculptor must have envisaged it as a single compact block rendered in vigorous rhythmic lines. It is clearly similar to Egyptian and Phoenician sarcophagi, or even the *xoana* of archaic Greece.

47. Etruscan art of the 6th century BC. Small cinerary urn with a dancing scene carved in relief. Museo Nazionale Archeologico, Palermo. The urn, carved from a block of sandstone, was found at Chiusi. In order to render the movements of the carved figures more supple, the sculptor has purposely distorted the proportions of their bodies into a pattern of flowing lines.

48. Etruscan art of the 6th and 5th centuries BC. *Warrior about to throw a spear.* Museo di Villa Giulia, Rome. Bronze figurines of this kind are common throughout Etruscan sculpture. Suppleness and poise are skilfully blended in the tensed muscles of the warrior's right arm.

49. Etruscan art of the 6th and 5th centuries BC. Bronze head of Acheloo. Museo di Villa Giulia, Rome. This was in all probability used to ornament a beam-end or a piece of furniture, and is typical of the Etruscans' liking for fanciful decoration — manifest, in this instance, in the full, flowing beard. Heads of this kind were made only in Tarquinia.

50. Etruscan art of the 6th century BC. *Woman Holding a Sucking Pig*. Museo di Villa Giulia, Rome. A bronze votive figurine discovered in the temple of Apollo at Veii; a finely carved piece. Notice the loose folds of the clothing and the slightly bent right leg, which are introduced to avoid excessive rigidity and verticality.

51. Etruscan art of the 6th century BC. Antefix in the shape of a Gorgon. Museo di Villa Giulia, Rome. The mask is one of the series of Gorgons, Sileni and maenads that were set on the roof cornices of the temple of Apollo at Veii. A halo like a shell frames the head, which is carved with simplicity and decorative elegance.

52. Etruscan art of the 6th century BC. Figurines of a warrior and a woman (36 cm). Museo Archeologico, Florence. These figurines, found at Brolio in the Chiana Valley, must once have been vase-supports. The compact surfaces, stylisation and use of geometrical volumes indicate that they were inspired by Cretan sculpture.

53. Etruscan art of the 6th century BC. *Mars*. Museo di Villa Giulia, Rome. The underlying geometrical principle in numerous bronze figurines made in Etruria between the 9th and 7th centuries BC, might lead one to believe that they had some sort of connection with Nuraghic sculpture in Sardinia. But the use of curved lines indicates that they were made much later.

54. Etruscan art of the 6th century BC. *Aeneas Carrying his Father Anchises on his Shoulders.* Museo di Villa Giulia, Rome. The clay votive group comprising Aeneas and his father Anchises was found in the temple of Apollo at Veii. The two figures are neatly dove-tailed, forming a perfectly balanced whole.

55. Etruscan art of the 6th and 5th centuries BC. Head of a warrior wearing an Attic helmet. Museo di Villa Giulia, Rome. This was found in the temple of Mater Matuta at Satricum, a Volscian city in the south of Latium; the temple functioned between the 7th and 2nd centuries BC. The head, encased in its helmet with bull's horns, had been detached from a facing slab moulded in high relief.

56. Etruscan art of the 6th century BC. Jug in the shape of a bull's head. Museo Archeologico, Florence. This terracotta jug is in a category by itself as regards form and proportions. It is an imitation of bronze models, in a decidedly surrealist manner. Lion heads and bull-tamers are moulded in relief.

57. Etruscan art of the 5th century BC. *Woman and Child* (90 cm). Museo Archeologico, Florence. Found at Chianciano; it is a later development of cinerary urns from Chiusi. Although Greek influence (Attic in particular) is evident, it also contains purely local characteristics — in this instance the fixed stare and the clumsy folds of the clothing.

58. Etruscan art of the 5th century BC. *Silenus.* Museo Archeologico, Florence. One of a series of three figurines on the lid of a brazier found at La Bonica, near Chiusi. The custom of ornamenting household objects with figurines of deities, warriors and animals was widespread in Etruria and elsewhere in Italy. As a result, bronze figurines became the commonest form of applied art.

59. Etruscan art of the 4th century BC. Handle of a cist (16 cm). Museo di Villa Giulia, Rome. Cists — round engraved bronze receptacles decorated with supports and lid-handles in the shape of figurines — were so popular in Etruria during the 4th century BC. that the toilet-set of a fashionable woman was not complete without one. A notable centre of production was Praeneste (Palestrina) in Latium. This group of three figurines — two warriors armed with spears who support a companion slain in battle — form the handle.

60. Etruscan art of the 4th and 3rd centuries BC. *Child Playing with a Bird.* Museo di Villa Giulia, Rome. The Etruscans appear to have been the first people to devise and develop the art of portraiture from life. This small terracotta figure from Vulci is at once a delightful portrait of a child and a refreshing piece of realistic observation.

61. Etruscan art of the 5th-3rd centuries BC. *Head of a smiling child*. Museo di Villa Giulia, Rome. Like the previous plate, an exquisitely graceful portrait of a child, also from Vulci. The child's features, lips barely parted in a smile, are rendered with realism softened by a touch of sentimentality.

62. Etruscan art of the 4th and 3rd centuries BC. *Woman with a Child in her Lap and a Cup in her Right Hand*. Museo di Villa Giulia, Rome. Small clay group from the temple of the Manganello at Cerveteri. It is worthy of notice principally because of the almost Baroque composition of lines and planes, splendidly balanced and executed with an incisive and vigorous Hellenistic exuberance.

63. Etruscan art of the 4th and 3rd centuries BC. Two elongated bronze figurines. The elongation of figurines is frequent in Etruscan sculpture during the 4th and 3rd centuries BC, and is perhaps a symptom of decadence. The practice may also be interpreted as an Etruscan reaction against the tide of Greek influence by the production of works that are the antithesis of naturalism.

64. Etruscan art of the 4th–2nd centuries BC. *Seated Couple.*
Museo di Villa Giulia, Rome. This votive group modelled in
clay was found at Satricum. Ino, called also 'Mater Matuta',
is here shown seated beside a young, bare-chested god. She is
modelled in an archaic manner not found in the lively secular
figurines dating from the same period.